MARK HARMON

BIOGRAPHY:

A Life In Character

Rooks Hill

Mark Harmon

Disclaimer:
The following book is for entertainment and informational purposes only.The stories, events, and dialogue recreated in this biography are based on extensive research, interviews, and the author's own interpretation of the available information.

Mark Harmon

TABLE OF CONTENTS

INTRODUCTION

CHAPTER 1: WHO IS MARK HARMON?

CHAPTER 2: EDUCATIONAL JOURNEY

CHAPTER 3: FROM FIELD TO FAME

CHAPTER 4: FINDING HIS FOOTING

CHAPTER 5: TV JOURNEY BEGINS

CHAPTER 6: STARRING IN ST. ELSEWHERE

CHAPTER 7: EMBRACING FILM

CHAPTER 8: ICONIC ROLES

CHAPTER 9: COLLABORATIONS WITH COLLEAGUES

CHAPTER 10: CHALLENGES AND TRIUMPHS

CHAPTER 11: GLOBAL RECOGNITIONS AND AWARDS

CHAPTER 12: FAMILY AND FAME

CONCLUSION

INTRODUCTION

Mark Harmon has always been a figure of quiet strength, a man who stands out not for loud theatrics but for his unwavering dedication and authenticity. His journey through Hollywood, unlike many, is defined not by scandals or the chase for fame but by a profound commitment to his craft. As an actor, he has captivated audiences with his ability to embody complex characters with a steady, nuanced presence, making him a favorite on screens across generations. Yet, what makes him remarkable is not just his career; it's the way he has carried himself through it all, holding fast to values of integrity, humility, and resilience.

One particular moment that captured the essence of who Harmon is came during an awards ceremony, where he stood before a packed room, accepting recognition for his role in shaping television history. The applause echoed throughout the hall, but even in the midst of acclaim, Harmon appeared almost uncomfortable with the spotlight. For him, this moment wasn't just about

personal achievement; it was a reflection of the hard
work, late nights, and countless collaborative efforts that
had gone into his projects. Harmon knew his success was
as much about those who worked beside him—the
writers, directors, co-stars, and crew members—as it was
about his own performances. It was in that moment that
his humility shone through, showcasing his deep respect
for the art form and the people behind it.

While many stars accept awards as symbols of individual
success, Harmon's approach was different. His quiet
words and gracious demeanor reflected a man who
didn't view his career as a series of accolades, but as a
journey built on purpose and responsibility. Harmon saw
acting as a privilege, a chance to tell meaningful stories
that touched lives. Throughout his career, he embraced
each role with an attitude of dedication, never one to
seek fame for fame's sake but rather to do justice to the
characters he portrayed.
As he stepped down from the stage that night, the room
was filled with a palpable respect, not only for the
award-winning actor but for the man himself, a person

who valued the relationships, the teamwork, and the quiet discipline that had carried him to this moment. For his fans, that evening was a reminder of why Mark Harmon remained an enduring figure in Hollywood: he was not just an actor but an example, someone who managed to stay true to himself amid the unpredictable tides of show business.

CHAPTER 1: WHO IS MARK HARMON?

Mark Harmon, a well-regarded figure in Hollywood known for his understated and grounded persona, was born Thomas Mark Harmon on September 2, 1951, in Burbank, California. Growing up in an environment that celebrated achievements in both sports and entertainment, Mark was introduced early on to values of dedication and resilience, qualities that would shape his life and career. His father, Tom Harmon, was a celebrated college football player who won the prestigious Heisman Trophy, later becoming a noted sports broadcaster. His mother, Elyse Knox, was a successful actress and fashion designer, blending artistry and style that brought her acclaim during Hollywood's golden era. With such accomplished parents, Mark inherited both athletic prowess and a flair for the performing arts, though his path to fame was uniquely his own.

Mark was the youngest of three children, growing up with two older sisters, Kristin and Kelly, each carving out their own spaces in entertainment. Kristin, the eldest, found her niche as an actress and painter, and Kelly became a model and actress, demonstrating the family's affinity for creativity and performance. Being the youngest in a high-achieving family, he observed and absorbed the skills and values around him, forming a well-rounded character with a mix of strength and sensitivity. His close-knit family fostered a deep sense of loyalty and integrity in him, qualities that would later become part of his public persona.

Standing at around 6 feet, Mark had an athletic build that perfectly suited his role as a quarterback, and his physique would later serve him well in his acting career, allowing him to portray characters with both strength and vulnerability.

While sports seemed like a natural career path, Mark felt a pull towards acting, an art he had long admired. He was drawn to the challenge of becoming different characters and telling their stories, something he found deeply meaningful. His transition from athlete to actor was not an abrupt shift but rather a thoughtful decision shaped by his experiences and family background. He began to explore opportunities in the entertainment industry, taking on small roles and working tirelessly to refine his skills. Over time, he discovered a passion for storytelling that went beyond the superficial aspects of fame. He valued the craft of acting itself, the preparation, the discipline, and the ability to connect with audiences. His career breakthrough came in television, where his ability to embody complex characters quickly caught the attention of viewers and industry insiders alike. Outside of acting, Mark Harmon has a variety of interests that reflect his multifaceted personality.

He enjoys outdoor activities, particularly carpentry and woodworking, which he finds both relaxing and creatively satisfying. Harmon has even built structures on his own property, finding joy in creating something tangible and lasting. His love for working with his hands is evident in his attention to detail and appreciation for craftsmanship, traits that parallel his approach to acting.

This hobby also highlights his down-to-earth nature, showing that he values the process of creating as much as the end result.

Harmon is also known for his love of sports, which he carries from his early days as an athlete. He enjoys watching football and other sports, keeping the competitive spirit alive in his personal life. Additionally, Mark is passionate about family, often choosing to spend his time away from the spotlight with his wife, actress Pam Dawber, and their two children. His commitment to his family is evident in his decision to keep his personal life private, focusing instead on maintaining a stable and nurturing environment for his loved ones.

Mark Harmon's physique and demeanor have always contributed to his presence on screen. Standing tall with a rugged build and chiseled features, he exudes a strength and reliability that make him an ideal fit for authoritative roles. His expressive blue eyes and steady gaze lend an authenticity to his characters, allowing him to portray a range of emotions, from quiet determination to deep vulnerability. These physical attributes, combined with his disciplined work ethic, have made him one of Hollywood's most respected actors. Despite his fame, he remains humble and grounded, often attributing his success to the support of his family and colleagues. He approaches his career with a strong sense of responsibility, respecting the work that goes into creating television and the impact it can have on audiences. For Harmon, acting is not about fame but about telling stories that resonate and inspire. This sense of purpose drives his commitment to his craft and keeps him focused on what matters most in life: authenticity, family, and hard work.

Through his career, Harmon has received numerous awards and accolades, but he views these recognitions as a testament to the collaborative nature of the projects he's worked on. He has always been quick to credit his co-stars, crew, and everyone involved in the production, seeing himself as part of a larger team. This attitude of humility and gratitude has endeared him to his colleagues and fans, making him a role model for aspiring actors and viewers alike. Mark Harmon's life is a story of balance between fame and privacy, ambition and humility, artistry and family values. He represents a type of Hollywood star that is rare, one who values substance over spectacle and remains dedicated to his principles. His career serves as a reminder that true success comes from staying true to oneself, embracing challenges, and never losing sight of what truly matters.

CHAPTER 2: EDUCATIONAL JOURNEY

Growing up in a family that valued both education and achievement, Mark Harmon developed a disciplined approach to learning from an early age. His parents, who had excelled in their respective fields, instilled in him the importance of hard work and the benefits of a well-rounded education. This foundation set him on a path that emphasized not only formal education but also personal growth and self-discipline.

His early school years took place in Los Angeles, where he attended a local elementary school. Here, he was exposed to a world of diverse subjects, and his inquisitive nature made him an engaged student. Even at a young age, he was observant and curious, keen to learn and explore new ideas. His parents encouraged him to focus on his studies, instilling in him the importance of balancing academics with other aspects of life, a lesson that would serve him well later on.

Mark Harmon

As Harmon transitioned into his teenage years, he enrolled at Harvard-Westlake School, an esteemed preparatory school in Los Angeles. Harvard-Westlake was known for its rigorous academics and competitive atmosphere, and attending this institution presented him with numerous opportunities to challenge himself. The school environment encouraged critical thinking and intellectual exploration, shaping his approach to education and problem-solving. It was here that he developed a strong work ethic, understanding the importance of preparation and focus—skills that would later translate into his career.

Harvard-Westlake placed a strong emphasis on athletics, and Harmon thrived in this dual environment of intellectual and physical growth. He became active in sports, particularly football, and began to discover his talent and interest in athletics. The school encouraged him to push his limits both on the field and in the classroom, fostering a balance between his intellectual and physical development. This balance became an integral part of his identity, one that he would carry forward into his adult life.

After completing high school, Harmon was faced with the decision of choosing a college. Given his athletic talent, he received interest from several colleges that wanted him to play football. He chose Pierce College in Woodland Hills, California, a community college where he could continue playing football while focusing on his studies. This decision reflected a practical approach; rather than rushing into a major university, he took a measured path that allowed him to hone his athletic skills while exploring his academic interests.

At Pierce College, he excelled on the football field, quickly establishing himself as a key player. His performances were notable, and he demonstrated the same dedication to his sport as he did to his studies. Pierce College offered him an environment where he could grow at his own pace, and it provided a stepping stone for what would come next in his educational and athletic journey. His success on the field attracted attention from major universities, and soon he had options for transferring to a four-year institution.

In his quest for both athletic and academic advancement, Harmon transferred to the University of California, Los

Angeles (UCLA), a decision that would define his college years. At UCLA, he took on the role of starting quarterback for the Bruins football team, a prestigious position that brought him both challenges and opportunities. Harmon's time at UCLA was a period of intense personal and academic growth. Balancing the rigorous demands of being a student-athlete required discipline and time management, skills that he developed throughout his time there.

Academically, UCLA provided Harmon with a wealth of resources and exposure to a broad range of subjects. The university's dynamic environment encouraged critical thinking, and he was able to explore his interests more deeply. While he maintained a strong commitment to his studies, his role as quarterback added an extra layer of responsibility. Being in a leadership position on the football team taught him valuable lessons about teamwork, strategy, and resilience, which would later prove invaluable in his career.

His studies at UCLA were diverse, allowing him to engage with subjects that piqued his interest and broadened his perspective. He was drawn to courses that required analytical thinking and problem-solving, areas that complemented his disciplined nature. Although balancing academics and athletics was demanding, Harmon demonstrated an unwavering commitment to both. He approached his studies with the same determination that he showed on the football field, embracing each challenge as an opportunity to grow.

In addition to academics and sports, his time at UCLA allowed Harmon to meet people from different backgrounds, enriching his understanding of the world. This exposure to diverse perspectives would later influence his acting career, where he became known for portraying characters with depth and authenticity. Harmon's educational journey at UCLA was not only about acquiring knowledge but also about developing a well-rounded personality that could adapt to various roles in life.

Upon graduating from UCLA, Harmon faced a crossroads, as he considered the possibility of a career in professional sports. However, he realized that his interests extended beyond athletics, and he wanted to explore other avenues. His educational experiences had given him a foundation in critical thinking and discipline, qualities that could be applied in numerous fields. With a degree in communications, he was equipped with skills that would be valuable in the entertainment industry, though at the time, he was unsure of the exact path he wanted to take.

Harmon's formal education ended with his college graduation, but his commitment to learning continued throughout his life. Even as he transitioned into acting, he approached the craft with the same dedication he had shown in school and sports. His educational background provided him with a strong sense of discipline and an analytical mindset, which he applied to each role he took on. Harmon's understanding of character dynamics and his ability to analyze scripts were skills he had honed through years of study and personal growth. Throughout his acting career, Harmon remained a lifelong learner, constantly seeking ways to improve his craft. He read extensively, researched his roles, and observed the work of other actors, always aiming to deepen his understanding of the profession. His educational journey had instilled in him a belief in the value of preparation and knowledge, which he applied to every project. This commitment to learning and self-improvement set him apart in the entertainment industry, where he became known for his thoughtful approach to acting.

Harmon's path through education was not a straight line, nor was it marked by a single passion or goal. Instead, it was a journey shaped by curiosity, resilience, and a desire to make the most of each opportunity. His experiences in school and college laid the groundwork for a successful career, teaching him the importance of perseverance and adaptability. Today, his life reflects the values he learned through his educational journey, a dedication to excellence, a respect for hard work, and an understanding of the importance of both intellectual and personal growth.

His educational background serves as a reminder that learning is not confined to the classroom; it is a lifelong process that continues with each new experience and challenge. Harmon's story is one of a man who valued his education not just as a means to an end but as a foundation for a fulfilling life. Through his journey, he shows that true success comes from a commitment to growth, both academically and personally, and that each step on the educational path contributes to the person one becomes.

CHAPTER 3: FROM FIELD TO FAME

Mark Harmon's rise from the football field to the Hollywood spotlight is a testament to versatility, hard work, and a relentless drive for excellence. This journey began with Harmon's passion for athletics, especially football, a sport that tested his physical limits and nurtured his competitive spirit. While many individuals strive to make it big in one field, Harmon's story reflects an ability to succeed in two contrasting arenas—sports and acting, both demanding unique skills and dedication. His early years on the football field served as a crucial foundation, helping him develop resilience, discipline, and teamwork. Football was more than just a sport for him; it was an environment where he learned to handle pressure and develop strategies for overcoming challenges. As a quarterback, Harmon had to be a quick thinker, anticipate the moves of opponents, and communicate effectively with his teammates. These skills not only made him successful in football but later proved invaluable in his acting career.

His athletic prowess earned him recognition, eventually leading him to a football scholarship at the University of California, Los Angeles (UCLA). UCLA provided Harmon with the chance to play on a larger stage, bringing him into the public eye and allowing him to refine his skills further. Playing as a quarterback for the UCLA Bruins required him to manage the dual responsibilities of being a college athlete and a student. Excelling in both roles, Harmon gained respect not only as an athlete but as an individual who could balance multiple demands. The rigor of collegiate sports taught him resilience and the value of relentless effort, setting the tone for the next phase of his life.

Despite the prospects of a professional sports career, Harmon decided to pursue a different path after college. He recognized that while football was a significant part of his identity, it wasn't his only passion. This decision to leave behind a promising athletic career and venture into acting may have seemed unexpected to many, but for Harmon, it was a natural evolution of his personal growth. The skills and values instilled in him on the field, perseverance, commitment, and adaptability were qualities that would serve him well in Hollywood.

Entering the entertainment industry was not an easy transition. Harmon was stepping into an entirely new world, one that required a different set of skills and exposed him to a highly competitive environment. Unlike the structured life of an athlete, acting presented constant changes and new challenges with every role. Yet, Harmon approached acting with the same level of discipline he had cultivated on the field. He spent hours studying the craft, learning from experienced actors, and absorbing every lesson he could. He understood that success in Hollywood required as much dedication and hard work as his years in sports.

Harmon's initial years in the acting world were characterized by perseverance and gradual progress. While he didn't achieve overnight fame, he remained committed to improving his craft, taking on various roles that allowed him to showcase his talent. His early work in television helped him gain experience, exposing him to the intricacies of performance, camera work, and character development. Each role, no matter how small, was an opportunity for growth, and Harmon made sure to learn from each experience.

As Harmon's acting career began to gain traction, his reputation as a reliable and versatile actor grew. He quickly became known for his ability to adapt to different roles, embodying each character with a depth and authenticity that resonated with audiences. His time as a quarterback had taught him the importance of leadership, and this trait translated well into his acting. Harmon brought a sense of responsibility and focus to his roles, treating each project with respect and dedication.

One of the defining moments in Harmon's career came when he landed a role on "St. Elsewhere", a popular medical drama series that showcased his talent and further established him in Hollywood. His portrayal in the series demonstrated his range as an actor, earning him critical acclaim and the admiration of viewers. This success was not a fluke; it was the result of years of consistent effort and a commitment to refining his craft. Harmon approached each scene with precision, drawing from his life experiences to bring authenticity to his character. This role marked a turning point, as it opened doors to more prominent opportunities in television and film.

Building on the success of "St. Elsewhere", he continued to make strategic choices in his career, selecting roles that allowed him to explore different aspects of his personality and abilities. His journey through Hollywood was not a linear path of success but a series of calculated moves and hard work. Each project he took on added to his skill set, and he became known not just as a talented actor but as someone who could handle a wide range of characters. His willingness to tackle challenging roles set him apart and added to his credibility as an actor.

In the early 2000s, Harmon took on what would become his most iconic role—as Leroy Jethro Gibbs in "NCIS". This role solidified his position in Hollywood and brought him widespread recognition. As Gibbs, Harmon displayed a level of commitment and intensity that captivated audiences and contributed to the show's immense popularity. Playing Gibbs allowed Harmon to blend the discipline he had developed in sports with the emotional depth he had cultivated as an actor. The role demanded not just talent but an understanding of complex character dynamics, something Harmon excelled at. His performance on "NCIS" resonated with fans and critics alike, establishing him as one of television's most respected actors.

Throughout his career, Harmon's approach to his work has remained consistent. Whether on the football field or in front of the camera, he has always valued preparation, integrity, and dedication. These qualities have allowed him to achieve success in two very different fields, showing that excellence is attainable with the right mindset and work ethic. His transition from sports to acting was not just a career shift but a testament to his adaptability and drive.

His journey from field to fame is an inspiring story of resilience and self-discovery. His path reminds us that success is not confined to a single domain; it is a product of determination and the willingness to embrace new challenges. His ability to navigate two contrasting worlds, sports and entertainment, speaks to his versatility and commitment to growth. Each phase of his life has contributed to the person he is today, a figure admired for his talent, humility, and dedication.

In Hollywood, where fame is often fleeting, Harmon's sustained success is a rare achievement. His career reflects a balance between ambition and authenticity, and his journey serves as an example of how pursuing one's passions with sincerity can lead to lasting fulfillment. From the lessons learned on the field to the experiences gathered in front of the camera, Harmon's life embodies the values of hard work, adaptability, and perseverance.

CHAPTER 4: FINDING HIS FOOTING

Navigating the unpredictable world of Hollywood requires more than just ambition. For someone starting out, it's a complex journey marked by fierce competition, steep learning curves, and relentless challenges. In the beginning, stepping into the entertainment industry can feel like entering an entirely new universe, one where expectations are high, and the stakes are even higher. For a young actor without connections, the path to recognition often demands a blend of skill, adaptability, and patience. Each role, however minor, serves as a critical opportunity to learn the nuances of the craft and the intricacies of the industry itself.

These initial steps can often involve taking on roles that aren't glamorous but provide invaluable experience. Many budding actors face an array of challenges, from navigating auditions to dealing with rejection. Each setback, however, becomes a lesson in resilience and an essential part of building character. In Hollywood, a performer's perseverance is often tested early on, as the reality of the industry reveals that success doesn't happen overnight. The path is typically dotted with moments of self-doubt and disappointment, but it's in these times that foundational lessons are learned.

For a fresh face in the industry, building credibility takes time and an unwavering commitment to improvement. The early days often involve a succession of small roles, which might feel thankless but are, in fact, crucial stepping stones. Gaining experience in front of the camera, however limited, contributes to an actor's confidence and helps refine their craft. Learning to embody different characters, however briefly, develops range and fosters an understanding of performance that only on-set experience can teach. For many, the early journey through Hollywood is as much about learning the craft as it is about self-discovery.

Mark Harmon's early steps in Hollywood were not the fast-track path to stardom that some might imagine. Like many aspiring actors, his journey was filled with challenges, setbacks, and a fair amount of perseverance before finding the success that would later define his career. Hollywood, with all its glitz and glamor, was a daunting world to break into, and Harmon, though talented, faced the reality of starting from the bottom. His early struggles were marked by the need to prove himself in a highly competitive environment where only the most persistent made it to the top.

When Harmon first arrived in Los Angeles, he was far from the household name he would eventually become. Despite his natural talent and an early desire to be an actor, he lacked the immediate connections or the big breaks that often help newcomers in Hollywood. His first steps were humble, and the challenges he faced were common for many starting out in the entertainment industry. Hollywood was a tough place, particularly for someone who wasn't part of the typical star-making machine, and Harmon's journey was no exception. Before his acting career even truly began, Harmon pursued other interests. Growing up in a family that valued education and discipline, Harmon initially thought about careers outside of acting. His passion for sports, particularly football, was something he considered more seriously in his younger years. It was only after exploring other options that he decided to focus fully on acting. However, making this transition was no easy feat, and entering Hollywood's highly competitive world of acting proved to be a lengthy and difficult process.

His first roles in Hollywood were small and often went unnoticed by the masses. Many early roles were guest spots on television shows or minor roles in films, which provided little more than exposure and experience. These roles didn't have the immediate spark to propel him into the spotlight, but they were crucial in honing his craft. Harmon's ability to make the most of these small parts, to deliver performances that were memorable even if brief, is a testament to his work ethic and determination. Although it may have seemed like an uphill battle, every experience added to his resume, and every role was a stepping stone in the long road to stardom. His early work was marked by a lack of immediate recognition, and this anonymity forced him to focus on improving his skills rather than seeking fame. This period in his life was not glamorous. It involved long hours of auditioning, dealing with rejection, and learning the intricacies of the industry. However, these early years were pivotal in shaping Harmon's approach to his career. He was determined to refine his craft, and with each audition, he learned more about the nuances of acting and how to make a lasting impression. His perseverance in the face of rejection is something that would define his career in the long run.

During this time, he also worked to carve out his unique identity within the industry. The entertainment world is often characterized by a search for the next big thing, but Harmon was never interested in fitting into a mold that didn't align with his personality or values. Instead of striving to be just another pretty face or action hero, he embraced roles that showcased his range and versatility. He was more interested in creating characters with depth

and substance, ones that would leave a lasting impact on
audiences.

As his career progressed, he found himself working with
more well-known directors and actors, and though many
of his early roles were not standout moments, they were
the training ground that helped him build his reputation.
These formative years helped him develop his natural
ability to connect with an audience. a skill that would
serve him well in later years. His experiences during this
period may not have yielded instant fame. but they laid
the foundation for his future success. He learned what it
took to survive in the industry and began to understand
the importance of persistence.

Despite the challenges, Harmon didn't lose sight of his
goal. His early years in Hollywood were not without
financial difficulties either. The instability of freelance
work, the long hours of auditioning, and the inconsistent
paychecks took a toll, and at times, Harmon wondered if
the sacrifices were worth it. But it was during this phase
that he learned resilience. Hollywood wasn't kind to
everyone, and not every actor made it through the rough

patches. But Harmon's determination to succeed helped him navigate those early years, and he began to notice the gradual growth in his career.

It wasn't just the hard work that set him apart, it was also his ability to build relationships within the industry. Early on, Harmon understood that in Hollywood, who you know could often matter just as much as what you know. He worked to cultivate connections with directors, producers, and fellow actors, knowing that a successful career is often built on a network of people who believe in your talent. Though he never sought fame through high-profile associations, his work ethic and steady professionalism earned him the respect of those around him, which would later prove invaluable.

Despite the slow start, Mark Harmon began to gain more recognition for his ability to take on serious roles that required both emotional depth and vulnerability. His portrayals of complex characters in both television and film showcased his versatility as an actor. While he was still far from the household name he would eventually become, the industry began to take notice. Directors and producers began to see his potential for more substantial roles, and his reputation as a talented actor began to grow. Still, it wasn't an overnight transformation. Success was gradual, and the journey remained one of slow and steady growth, rather than immediate fame.

Throughout this period, Harmon also began to recognize the value of persistence. He saw how many actors entered Hollywood with dreams of quick success, only to be derailed by the harsh realities of the industry. But he refused to give up. He didn't expect a sudden break or instant fame. Instead, he focused on developing his skills, learning from each experience, and positioning himself for long-term success. His approach to his early years in Hollywood was rooted in patience. He knew it was only a matter of time before his work would pay off, and he stayed committed to the process, trusting that his dedication would eventually lead to recognition. Ultimately, Mark Harmon's first steps in Hollywood were marked by the qualities of perseverance, dedication, and resilience. It was through his early struggles and challenges that he built the foundation for his future career. These early experiences helped him to understand the realities of the industry, to refine his acting skills, and to develop the strong work ethic that would define his entire career. His journey from anonymity to stardom was long and often difficult, but it was through those struggles that he truly found his footing in Hollywood.

CHAPTER 5: TV JOURNEY BEGINS

Beginning a career in television often marks a significant shift for actors, as they step into a medium that demands adaptability and consistency, and allows them to reach audiences directly in their homes. The television industry offers a unique blend of storytelling opportunities, with serial formats that let characters evolve and allow viewers to form deeper connections. For many actors, entering television is both an exciting and daunting endeavor, as it combines rigorous schedules, high expectations, and the challenge of captivating audiences week after week.

Television roles require a different approach from those in film, as characters are developed and explored over multiple episodes or seasons. This gradual build allows actors to reveal layers of their characters slowly, bringing complexity and depth to their portrayals. The need to engage viewers continually means that the actor must invest deeply in their role, embodying the character's traits in a way that remains fresh yet consistent across episodes. This can be challenging, as television schedules are demanding, often requiring actors to balance long hours on set with the personal commitment to maintaining energy and authenticity in each scene.

When starting in television, actors may begin with smaller parts, which are still essential for gaining experience and establishing a reputation. Supporting roles often introduce actors to the pacing of TV production, which moves quickly and sometimes involves shooting multiple scenes in a day. This fast pace teaches the importance of preparation, as there is limited time for rehearsals or reshoots. Actors learn to rely on their instincts, drawing from their training to make quick adjustments based on direction, which sharpens their skills and builds confidence.

Television also brings the opportunity to work with various directors and writers, each bringing unique insights and styles to the production. This collaborative environment can be an enriching experience for actors, who benefit from adapting to different creative visions. These interactions allow actors to gain new perspectives, as each director may have a distinct way of interpreting scenes or guiding performances. For an actor, this exposure is invaluable, as it broadens their understanding of the craft and prepares them to handle diverse roles in future projects.

Mark Harmon's transition into television marked a pivotal moment in his career, setting him on the path to becoming a household name. Television, with its fast-paced demands and ever-evolving landscape, offered him a platform to showcase his talents to a wide audience. Although he had already made some strides in Hollywood, television gave him the opportunity to expand his range, take on complex roles, and ultimately gain recognition in ways that film could not provide at the time.

Harmon's television career began in the 1970s, after a few years of trying to establish himself in Hollywood. His first notable roles were in guest appearances on various shows, which helped introduce him to the TV industry. While these roles were brief, they allowed him to develop his craft, adapt to the nuances of television acting, and begin building relationships within the industry. However, his early appearances did not immediately catapult him into stardom. Instead, they laid the foundation for what would eventually become a highly successful television career.

One of his early breakthrough moments came with his role on the medical drama "St. Elsewhere". The series, which aired from 1982 to 1988, became a significant turning point for Harmon, marking his entry into a world of long-term, recurring roles. Playing Dr. Robert Caldwell, a talented but often emotionally complex character, showcased his ability to tackle both drama and the human elements of healthcare professionals. "St. Elsewhere" was a critical success and earned praise for its intelligent storytelling and memorable performances. It was during this period that Harmon began to gain recognition for his on-screen presence and solidified his place in television history.

While "St. Elsewhere" was the first major role that brought him attention, Harmon's success on the show was not without its challenges. The show's complex narrative structure and sometimes experimental approach to storytelling required Harmon to take risks as an actor. He was tasked with portraying a character who was layered and multifaceted, and this pushed him to explore new depths in his acting.

Despite the accolades Harmon received during this time, his career was far from a smooth ascent. Like many actors in television, Harmon had to contend with the industry's constant pressure to succeed. The entertainment world is known for its fleeting nature, where success is often short-lived, and even accomplished actors can find themselves without work. Harmon, however, proved his resilience in the face of these pressures. His experiences during the *St. Elsewhere* years taught him valuable lessons about the unpredictability of the television industry and how to maintain his focus on the craft rather than on the fleeting nature of fame. After "St. Elsewhere" concluded, his television journey did not come to an immediate halt. Instead, he embraced new opportunities, working on a variety of projects that allowed him to continue evolving as an actor. These included guest spots on various TV series and roles in made-for-television films. Although none of these projects became as iconic as his time on "St. Elsewhere", they allowed him to demonstrate his versatility as an actor and helped him stay visible in the competitive world of television. Harmon's adaptability became one of his defining traits. Rather than sticking to one genre or type of role, he sought out parts that challenged him and expanded his range.

A significant milestone in Harmon's television career came in the early 2000s with the role of Leroy Jethro Gibbs on the long-running procedural drama "NCIS". This role would go on to define much of his television legacy. Playing the stoic and highly skilled Special Agent Gibbs, Harmon became the face of a show that would captivate audiences for years. "NCIS" quickly became one of the most popular television series, and Harmon's portrayal of Gibbs was a driving force behind its success. The character, known for his no-nonsense attitude and complex backstory, resonated with viewers, and Harmon's portrayal was praised for its depth and consistency.

The success of "NCIS" was not an overnight phenomenon, and it took time for the show to find its footing in the television landscape. Harmon's steady performance and commitment to the role of Gibbs were crucial in maintaining the show's tone and emotional core, even through changes in the cast and shifts in the storylines. As the series progressed, Harmon's character became a beloved figure, and his reputation as a leading man in television was firmly established. His portrayal of Gibbs became a model for future TV detectives and reinforced his position as one of the most respected actors in the industry.

The rigorous production schedule, the need for emotional range, and the pressure to maintain high viewer ratings were constant challenges, but Harmon embraced these demands, knowing that his dedication was key to the show's success.

Another aspect of his television career that helped solidify his status as a respected figure was his ability to collaborate with a wide range of colleagues, from directors to fellow actors. Harmon was known for his professionalism on set, his willingness to mentor younger actors, and his strong work ethic. These qualities endeared him to his co-stars and crew members, who respected him not only for his acting but also for his leadership and team-oriented approach to the production process. It wasn't just his talent that made him successful in television; it was also his ability to foster a positive and collaborative working environment.

Throughout his career, Harmon demonstrated an unwavering commitment to his work. He showed that television, with all its challenges, could also provide an opportunity for actors to make a lasting impact. His journey in television was not one of instant fame or easy success but one that involved hard work, persistence, and an unrelenting drive to improve. Harmon's ability to navigate the ups and downs of the television world, while consistently delivering strong performances, was a testament to his resilience as an actor.

In the years following his success on "NCIS", he remained an influential figure in television, further proving that his role as Gibbs was just one chapter in a long and successful career. His time in television has solidified his legacy not just as an actor but as a fixture of American popular culture. With his ability to consistently choose compelling roles, work with talented directors and writers, and build strong relationships with his colleagues, Harmon's television journey became one that shaped the way audiences viewed both him and the medium itself.

Mark Harmon's television career is a testament to his dedication, versatility, and ability to navigate the challenges of the entertainment industry.

CHAPTER 6: STARRING IN ST. ELSEWHERE

Taking on a role in "St. Elsewhere" was a significant turning point for many actors, offering them a unique platform in one of the era's most respected television dramas. This medical drama was set in the fictional St. Eligius Hospital, a place often humorously referred to as "St. Elsewhere" by its staff, hinting at its reputation as a rundown facility where other hospitals would send difficult or "hopeless" cases. The show aired in the 1980s, a time when television was beginning to explore more complex, realistic themes and character arcs that challenged viewers' perceptions. "St. Elsewhere" quickly became a respected name in the TV landscape, breaking from traditional, straightforward hospital dramas to present a grittier, more nuanced portrayal of life in an urban hospital.

The series was known for its ensemble cast, which meant each actor had the opportunity to develop their character within a rich tapestry of stories. Unlike shows that focu heavily on a single protagonist, *St. Elsewhere* allowed multiple characters to shine, creating a dynamic environment where actors could fully immerse themselves in their roles. The depth of character development was a primary draw for actors, as it enabled them to play not just doctors and nurses but fully formed individuals grappling with both personal and professional challenges. Each character brought a unique perspective to the story, adding layers of complexity to the overall narrative.

Portraying a character on "St. Elsewhere" required an understanding of the gritty reality of hospital life. The show did not shy away from depicting the ethical dilemmas, emotional struggles, and grueling schedules faced by healthcare workers. For the actors, this meant fully embracing the gravity of their roles, as they had to convey both the dedication and the vulnerabilities of medical professionals. Playing these roles was a demanding experience, as the actors needed to balance moments of high-intensity drama with subtler, more introspective scenes that revealed their characters' inner struggles. This approach to storytelling was groundbreaking for the time, as it allowed audiences to see doctors as flawed yet resilient human beings.

Mark Harmon's role in "St. Elsewhere" marked a pivotal moment in his career, elevating him from a relatively unknown actor to one recognized for his exceptional talent and versatility. "St. Elsewhere" was not only a groundbreaking medical drama but also one of the shows that defined the 1980s television landscape. It was known for its compelling storytelling, complex characters, and innovative approach to television, and Harmon's portrayal of Dr. Robert Caldwell became an integral part of its success.

The series, which ran from 1982 to 1988, focused on the daily lives of the doctors, nurses, and staff at St. Eligius Hospital, a fictional medical institution in Boston. Unlike other medical dramas at the time, "St. Elsewhere" was not merely about the medical cases or hospital politics; it delved deeply into the personal lives and struggles of its characters. Mark Harmon's character, Dr.

Caldwell, was a young, talented doctor who was often portrayed as serious and hardworking but also dealing with his own set of emotional and professional challenges. Harmon's ability to portray the nuances of his character set him apart, allowing him to gain respect from both his co-stars and the audience.

One of the significant aspects of Mark Harmon's role was his ability to embody a character who was both complex and relatable. Dr. Caldwell was not a perfect character; he had flaws and imperfections, just like any real person. Harmon's portrayal brought a level of humanity and authenticity to the role, something that resonated deeply with viewers. His performance was subtle but powerful, showcasing a range of emotions, from vulnerability to strength. This complexity helped Harmon stand out among the ensemble cast, which included notable actors such as Ed Begley Jr., William Daniels, and Howie Mandel.

Working alongside such a talented group of actors was both a challenge and a tremendous learning opportunity for Harmon. The cast of "St. Elsewhere" was made up of a diverse mix of established actors and newcomers, each bringing their own unique skills to the table. Harmon, however, quickly earned his place as one of the show's leading performers. The dynamic between him and his co-stars, especially his interactions with William Daniels, who played Dr. Mark Craig, was a highlight of the show. Daniels' portrayal of a brilliant yet egotistical surgeon was a perfect foil to Harmon's more grounded and empathetic character. Their on-screen relationship, marked by moments of tension and mutual respect, was one of the key elements that made "St. Elsewhere" so engaging.

The challenges that Harmon faced on this set were not limited to the emotional and dramatic complexities of his character. The show was known for its fast-paced production schedule and the constant pressure to deliver high-quality performances week after week. Harmon, like his colleagues, had to navigate long hours on set, dealing with the physical and emotional demands of portraying a doctor in a high-stakes medical environment. This was particularly challenging because the show often tackled heavy, emotionally charged storylines, such as death, illness, and personal loss. Harmon had to strike a delicate balance between portraying a medical professional who could empathize with patients while also showcasing his character's internal struggles. The show's realistic and often gritty portrayal of hospital life required Harmon to remain fully committed to his role, maintaining the emotional intensity needed for the drama.

Moreover, "St. Elsewhere" was a series that was not afraid to take risks with its narrative. The show frequently pushed boundaries, exploring themes such as mental illness, ethical dilemmas, and the darker aspects of human nature. For Harmon, this meant embracing a wide range of emotions and tackling controversial issues, which was a departure from some of the more traditional roles he had taken on before. At times, this required him to make difficult decisions as an actor, stepping outside his comfort zone and challenging his own abilities. The emotional toll that these storylines took on the cast was considerable, but Harmon's professionalism and dedication to his craft helped him navigate these moments with grace.

Another challenge Harmon faced was the ensemble nature of the series. With such a large and talented cast, there was always the risk that some actors would be overshadowed by their co-stars. However, Harmon managed to carve out a unique space for himself on the show, gaining recognition for his consistent performances and ability to hold his own against the other actors. While the show's storylines often centered on the doctors' relationships with each other and their patients, Harmon's character remained a constant presence, offering a sense of stability and reliability in the chaos of the hospital setting.

While "St. Elsewhere" was critically acclaimed, it was not without its challenges in terms of ratings and audience reception. Despite the critical success of the show, it never quite achieved the same level of mass popularity as other medical dramas of the time. However, the show's impact on the industry was undeniable. It paved the way for future medical dramas and set a new standard for how television could tackle serious and often controversial topics. Mark Harmon's role on the show became an important part of the series' legacy, and it helped him build a strong foundation for his future success in both television and film.

As the series came to an end in 1988, Harmon had already made his mark on the television industry. The show had provided him with valuable experience, not only in terms of acting but also in learning how to navigate the complexities of the television business. Harmon's ability to take on a complex character like Dr. Caldwell and turn it into a memorable and impactful role demonstrated his range as an actor. His performance laid the groundwork for the roles that would follow in his career, and it proved that Harmon was not just another television actor; he was someone with the potential to carry a show and bring depth to every character he portrayed.

CHAPTER 7: EMBRACING FILM

As the television industry continued to offer new and exciting opportunities, Mark Harmon began to expand his horizons beyond the small screen, looking toward the world of film. Although he had already established himself as a familiar face in the realm of television, Harmon felt a compelling need to take on challenges that would push him to grow as an actor. Transitioning from television to film, however, was not a seamless shift, and it involved a set of unique obstacles that required Harmon to adapt his craft to a new medium.

The film industry operates on a different scale compared to television, both in terms of production timelines and the types of roles offered. Film projects often involve a more condensed shooting schedule, where every scene is meticulously planned, and the stakes are often higher. With fewer opportunities to stretch a character over multiple episodes or seasons, actors must rely on conveying a character's essence within a limited timeframe. For Harmon, this required a new approach to acting. He had to master the art of making an impact in a short period, balancing emotional depth with brevity. Each scene in a film carries greater weight, and Harmon understood the need to adjust his performances accordingly.

One of the biggest hurdles he faced in his move to film was the shift in the type of roles he was being offered. Harmon had become well known for his steady portrayal of characters on television, often playing professionals in intense, dramatic settings. In films, however, the range of roles was much broader, and Harmon found himself competing for parts with many other established actors. The transition required him to prove that he could embody characters that were as rich and compelling as the ones he had portrayed on television. He needed to establish his place in an industry filled with actors who were just as hungry for success.

Despite these challenges, Harmon embraced the opportunity to showcase his versatility. His desire to explore different genres and characters in a new environment led him to accept various film roles, ranging from drama to comedy. These roles were often quite different from the ones he had grown accustomed to on television, but Harmon believed in the importance of challenging himself. In the process, he sought to step outside of the comfort zone that television work had afforded him and dive into roles that tested his abilities. For him, each film project represented an opportunity to push the boundaries of his craft and prove to himself and his fans that he could thrive in different settings.

While navigating the competitive nature of the film industry, Harmon had to confront the reality of not always being in the spotlight. Hollywood was an ever-changing landscape, and getting cast in major films was not always guaranteed. As a result, Harmon had to be persistent and patient. He had to work through periods when the film projects didn't come as quickly or as easily as he would have liked. During these times, he focused on honing his craft, ensuring that when the next opportunity arose, he would be ready. This experience taught him the importance of resilience and the value of perseverance, even when things weren't moving at the pace he had hoped for.

The experience of moving into film also brought a significant shift in the dynamics of his working relationships. On film sets, actors often have shorter shooting schedules, and the time spent with co-stars is much more condensed compared to television. This change meant that Harmon had to quickly forge strong connections with other actors and directors in a relatively short period of time. Unlike television, where relationships could develop and evolve over many weeks and months, films demanded that these bonds be formed quickly and efficiently. Harmon approached this challenge by relying on his extensive experience in the industry, drawing on his ability to collaborate effectively with others. This ability to quickly connect with fellow actors and directors would prove invaluable as he began to take on more complex roles in the years to come.

As Harmon continued his journey in the film industry, he found that the skills he had developed from years of television acting were not only transferable but essential in helping him thrive in this new arena. His experience in portraying multi-dimensional characters on television allowed him to approach his film roles with a depth that set him apart from others. Harmon's commitment to understanding his characters and delivering nuanced performances gave him the ability to bring authenticity to his roles, whether in comedy or drama.

However, his journey in the world of film wasn't without its personal challenges. While he was able to land roles in films, the industry's demands and the pressures to succeed weighed heavily on him. He had moments when he questioned whether the risks he was taking in film would pay off. But through each experience, he grew more confident in his abilities. Each project he took on helped him build a deeper understanding of the craft of filmmaking. He learned how to work within the unique constraints of film production while still allowing room for creativity and expression. These challenges only fueled his passion for acting, and Harmon became more determined to continue pursuing opportunities that allowed him to grow both personally and professionally.

Despite these challenges, Harmon's continued work in film helped cement his reputation as a talented and versatile actor. He began to be recognized for his ability to seamlessly transition from television to film, proving that his talents were not limited to one medium. His dedication to his craft, as well as his willingness to take on difficult and diverse roles, earned him respect from both his peers and audiences. Harmon had found his footing in the film industry, and his journey was a testament to the power of perseverance and adaptability in an industry known for its unpredictability.

The diversity of roles that Harmon embraced also spoke to his passion for storytelling. He was not just acting for the sake of fame or recognition; he was deeply invested in bringing new characters to life and contributing to stories that resonate with audiences. Whether the role required him to play a dramatic lead, a supporting character, or a comedic foil, Harmon always approached his work with the same dedication and care. His commitment to bringing honesty and realism to his performances helped set him apart in a competitive industry.

Through his journey in the film industry, Harmon learned to balance ambition with humility, understanding that success was not always immediate but earned through consistent effort and growth. Each film he worked on became another step in his evolution as an actor. Whether the project was successful or not, Harmon viewed every experience as an opportunity to refine his craft. This approach allowed him to build a career that was both fulfilling and enduring.

In the years to come, Mark Harmon would continue to embrace new film opportunities, using each one as a platform to demonstrate his commitment to his craft and his willingness to take on diverse challenges. Through his work, Harmon proved that an actor's journey is not simply about achieving fame but about continually evolving, exploring new avenues, and creating art that resonates with audiences. His foray into film was an important chapter in his career, one that would lead to greater recognition and success.

CHAPTER 8: ICONIC ROLES

Mark Harmon's career has been defined by a variety of roles that showcase his versatility as an actor. From his early days in television to his more recent work in popular series, Harmon has built a reputation for his ability to embody characters across different genres. His journey has been marked by the evolution of roles that challenged him, broadened his acting range, and, ultimately, cemented his status as one of Hollywood's most reliable and respected talents.

Harmon's breakout role came in the early 1980s when he was cast in the medical drama "St. Elsewhere". Playing Dr. Robert Caldwell, a kind and compassionate physician, Harmon quickly won the hearts of audiences with his authentic portrayal. While the role was relatively brief, it provided Harmon with his first major exposure on television and laid the foundation for his future career in acting. His performance was widely praised for its sensitivity and depth, qualities that would continue to define his future roles. While "St.

Elsewhere" offered Harmon early fame, it was his subsequent roles that began to carve out his distinctive career. One of the most notable of these roles came in the form of "Chicago Hope", another medical drama, where Harmon played Dr. Jack McNeil. This time, he stepped into the shoes of a troubled but brilliant surgeon grappling with personal and professional challenges. His performance was widely celebrated for its ability to convey vulnerability, intelligence, and emotional conflict. The show, which aired in the 1990s, became a critical success and garnered Harmon numerous accolades. His portrayal of Dr. McNeil showed his ability to take on complex roles and made it clear that he was more than capable of carrying a series. He was no longer just a pretty face; he was an actor who could tap into deep emotional reservoirs and deliver performances that resonated with viewers.

Despite Harmon's success on medical dramas, he was never one to be typecast. In the early 2000s, he ventured into new territory with a role that would solidify his legacy in the acting world: Leroy Jethro Gibbs in

"NCIS". This character became one of the most iconic roles of his career, earning Harmon a dedicated fan base and critical acclaim. As the gruff, no-nonsense leader of a team of special agents, Harmon's Gibbs was a far cry from the kind-hearted doctors he had previously portrayed. Instead of healing with a stethoscope, Gibbs used his sharp mind and investigative skills to solve crimes. Yet, beneath his tough exterior, Gibbs was a man deeply affected by the losses he had experienced in his life, especially the death of his family. This layered portrayal earned Harmon praise for his ability to balance the character's tough, authoritative persona with moments of deep, raw emotion. Gibbs became a household name, and Harmon's steady, reliable performance contributed to "NCIS" becoming one of the longest-running and most successful TV shows in history. His portrayal of Gibbs was a masterclass in understated acting, where every glance, every line of dialogue, and every interaction conveyed more than words could say.

While "NCIS" became the pinnacle of Harmon's television career, it was not the only role that showcased his diverse talents. In addition to his more well-known performances, he also took on a range of interesting roles in films. Throughout his career, Harmon appeared in several films, ranging from comedies to thrillers, and each role helped expand his acting range. For example, his portrayal of a supportive yet understated character in the 1986 film "Summer School" marked a departure from his usual serious roles. Playing the role of a laid-back gym teacher who steps in to teach a summer school class, Harmon displayed his comedic timing and ability to handle lighter, more humorous material. This role was an interesting contrast to his more intense, dramatic performances and proved that Harmon was more than capable of tackling roles in different genres.

Another film role that highlighted Harmon's versatility came in "The Presidio" (1988), where he starred alongside Sean Connery. Playing a San Francisco police officer investigating a military crime, Harmon took on a more action-packed role, demonstrating his ability to

portray a character who was both physically and
mentally strong. The role presented Harmon with an
opportunity to show off his action-star chops, and his
portrayal of the tough, morally upright officer was both
thrilling and captivating. While "The Presidio" was not a
massive hit, it reinforced Harmon's ability to navigate
different roles across a variety of settings and genres.

Harmon's ability to adapt to diverse characters continued
to be a hallmark of his career in television and film. In
the 1991 film "Fear and Loathing in Las Vegas",
Harmon played a more unconventional role as a
journalist on an outrageous adventure with Hunter S.
Thompson. His appearance in the film, although brief,
was yet another example of his range and commitment to
playing characters in out-of-the-ordinary situations. This
role further emphasized Harmon's willingness to take on
roles that challenged him, even if they fell outside the
traditional mainstream roles typically offered to him.
Despite the ups and downs in his early film career, it was
his sustained presence on television that would define
Harmon's legacy. The role of Leroy Jethro Gibbs, for

example, continued to draw attention for its subtle, yet powerful emotional depth. Gibbs' calm, decisive nature was the cornerstone of "NCIS", but Harmon's portrayal of the character's vulnerability was what made him truly memorable. His ability to reveal layers of the character's backstory without overtly expressing them made Gibbs a nuanced and enduring figure on television. His long-running success in "NCIS" led to Harmon becoming a pop culture icon, with his character often referred to as one of the best-loved TV personalities of the 21st century.

Through all his roles, Mark Harmon showed a deep commitment to his craft and a dedication to playing characters that resonate with audiences on a personal level. Whether portraying a doctor, a police officer, or a tough, yet tender team leader, Harmon continuously impressed with his ability to breathe life into his characters. He was never satisfied with simply playing a role; instead, he sought to infuse every character with depth, authenticity, and emotional resonance. His career has been a testament to his versatility, and the roles he has portrayed remain some of the most memorable in television and film.

His performances have consistently been recognized for their emotional depth and understated brilliance. He has become a symbol of professionalism in the entertainment industry, able to adapt to any role and bring it to life with authenticity and skill. Mark Harmon's career has been a journey of embracing new challenges, evolving with each role, and leaving a lasting impression on audiences around the world. Whether on television or in film, his iconic roles have shaped his career and have ensured that he remains a respected and beloved figure in Hollywood for years to come.

CHAPTER 9:

COLLABORATIONS WITH

COLLEAGUES

Mark Harmon's career has been significantly shaped by the relationships he has fostered with his colleagues, both on and off-screen. Throughout his journey in Hollywood, he has consistently demonstrated a remarkable ability to collaborate with a wide range of actors, directors, and producers, contributing to the success of many projects. His professionalism, respect for others, and dedication to his craft have made him a sought-after co-star, and his collaborations have often led to some of his most iconic performances.

One of the most notable aspects of Mark Harmon's career is the strong rapport he has built with his fellow cast members. This is particularly evident in his work on "NCIS", where he has spent over a decade working with a talented ensemble cast. The chemistry between

Harmon and his co-stars has been one of the key factors in the show's incredible longevity and success. His portrayal of Leroy Jethro Gibbs, a role that demands both emotional depth and authority, has been complemented by the performances of his colleagues, creating a dynamic that resonates with viewers. In particular, the chemistry between Harmon and Pauley Perrette, who played Abby Sciuto, has been widely praised. Their on-screen friendship, which evolved over the years, became a cornerstone of the show. Perrette's bubbly, eccentric character was often the perfect counterbalance to Harmon's stoic and serious Gibbs, and the contrast between their personalities added layers of richness to the show's storytelling. Harmon's ability to play off of Perrette's energy, while also offering moments of gravitas, demonstrated his versatility and ease with working in a collaborative environment.

Harmon has also enjoyed successful partnerships with other "NCIS" cast members. Michael Weatherly, who portrayed Tony DiNozzo, became one of Harmon's closest friends on set. Their on-screen relationship was filled with banter, mutual respect, and genuine camaraderie. Weatherly's humorous portrayal of DiNozzo often served as the comic relief, offering a lighthearted balance to Harmon's more serious Gibbs. The dynamic between the two characters helped solidify the show's success and made their partnership one of the most beloved on television. The friendship and trust between the actors extended beyond the set, with both Harmon and Weatherly speaking highly of one another in interviews and expressing their mutual admiration for each other's work.

Similarly, the professional rapport Harmon built with other "NCIS" actors such as Cote de Pablo, who portrayed Ziva David, and Sean Murray, who played Timothy McGee, played a significant role in the success of the show. Harmon's ability to work with a range of personalities and acting styles was one of the reasons "NCIS" became a hit, as the ensemble cast worked seamlessly together. Harmon, who often took on a mentor role within the group, was respected by his colleagues for his calm demeanor, leadership skills, and willingness to lend support to those around him. His approach to working with others fostered a positive and productive atmosphere on set, making it a highly collaborative environment where all actors felt valued and respected.

Beyond "NCIS", Harmon has worked with a variety of other actors on different projects throughout his career. Similarly, his collaboration with actors in films also showcased his adaptability and willingness to work in different environments.

In the 1991 film "The Presidio", Harmon starred alongside Sean Connery, a legendary actor with whom he shared the screen in a tense military thriller. Although Harmon was relatively young at the time, his interactions with Connery were notable for their respect and professionalism. The opportunity to work with a figure of Connery's stature helped Harmon expand his acting range and learn from an actor who had decades of experience in the industry. Connery's calm and measured approach to his craft was something that Harmon admired, and it influenced the way he approached his own roles in the future.

His collaborations with directors have also been instrumental in shaping his career. He has worked with some of the most respected directors in television and film, learning from their expertise and contributing to their vision in ways that have elevated the projects they have worked on. In his television career, Harmon's work with "NCIS" creator Donald Bellisario" stands out as one of the most significant partnerships. Bellisario, who created "NCIS" as a spinoff of "JAG", recognized Harmon's potential as an actor early on and brought him on board to play the role of Gibbs. Bellisario's guidance helped Harmon refine the character, and the director-actor collaboration was key to the development of the series. Harmon's ability to connect with Bellisario and bring the character of Gibbs to life was instrumental in the show's success, and their ongoing partnership throughout the years helped keep the series fresh and engaging.

Harmon has also worked with many other talented directors throughout his career, each bringing their own unique vision to the projects. On the set of "Chicago Hope", a medical drama that aired in the 1990s, Harmon collaborated with director Rod Holcomb. The show provided Harmon with the opportunity to work with a new ensemble cast and explore a different kind of character. Holcomb's direction helped Harmon delve into the complexities of his character, Dr. Jack McNeil, and the success of the series was, in part, a result of the strong working relationship between the actor and director. Harmon's flexibility and willingness to trust his directors have made him a favorite among many in the industry, as he is known for his ability to take direction and enhance the material.

Mark Harmon's approach to working with colleagues extends beyond the set, as he has always been a highly regarded figure in the entertainment industry. Colleagues often speak of his generosity and humility, noting that he is always willing to offer advice or lend a helping hand to those who need it. His reputation as a mentor and team player has made him a beloved figure among his peers, and his professionalism is something that has made him a constant presence in the industry for decades. The lasting relationships Harmon has built with his co-stars, directors, and producers have been key to his enduring success, and they continue to shape his career to this day.

As he continues to work in television and film, the impact of his collaborations remains evident. His ability to connect with other actors, directors, and producers has played a vital role in his career, and it is clear that his success is not just a result of his talent, but also of the strong relationships he has built with those around him. Through his work on "NCIS" and other projects, Harmon has demonstrated the power of collaboration, and it is this spirit that has contributed to his lasting legacy in Hollywood. His career is a testament to the value of teamwork, mutual respect, and the importance of building lasting, meaningful relationships in the entertainment industry.

CHAPTER 10: CHALLENGES AND TRIUMPHS

Throughout his illustrious career, Mark Harmon has faced numerous challenges, each of which has shaped him into the actor and person he is today. While his journey has been filled with notable successes and accomplishments, it has not been without its trials. The path to fame, particularly in Hollywood, is rarely straightforward, and Mark Harmon's story is no exception. His ability to overcome these obstacles and persevere through difficult times is a testament to his resilience, work ethic, and deep passion for his craft. One of the most significant challenges Harmon encountered early in his career was navigating the competitive and often unpredictable nature of the entertainment industry. As a young actor, he faced the tough reality of an industry that can sometimes be unkind to newcomers. Hollywood is notoriously difficult for aspiring actors to break into, and even those with natural talent and potential are often overlooked. Harmon's early years were marked by a series of auditions and small roles that didn't always lead to the career-making opportunities he sought. It wasn't an easy start, and many others in his position would have given up, but Harmon was determined to make his mark.

Despite facing setbacks in the beginning, Harmon found that perseverance and a willingness to learn were key to overcoming the early hurdles of his career. He worked tirelessly to hone his skills, choosing roles that would challenge him and allow him to grow as an actor. In some ways, the early struggles he faced allowed him to build the mental fortitude that would serve him well in the future. While many actors would have been discouraged by rejections and small parts, Harmon embraced each experience as an opportunity to develop his craft. His commitment to improvement and his refusal to give up ultimately paid off, as he began landing more significant roles.

However, the journey to success was not without its personal challenges. Like many in the industry, Harmon has had to balance the demands of a high-profile career with his private life. As an actor with increasing visibility, the pressure to maintain a public image while staying true to himself became another challenge. Hollywood often places actors under a microscope, scrutinizing every aspect of their lives. This intense public focus can be draining, and finding a balance between personal and professional life is not always easy. For someone like Harmon, who values privacy and tends to keep his personal life out of the spotlight, navigating this balance was particularly difficult. He faced the challenge of being in the public eye while attempting to maintain the privacy that was important to him and his family. His ability to handle this pressure while maintaining his integrity and composure is something that has set him apart from many of his peers.

Another challenge that Harmon faced was the physical demands of his career, especially in his later years. Playing the tough and stoic character of Leroy Jethro Gibbs on "NCIS" required him to not only deliver emotionally charged performances but also to engage in physically demanding scenes. The role often involved action-packed sequences, which required Harmon to stay in top physical condition. While he had previously enjoyed playing sports, the rigorous physical nature of his work on "NCIS" presented new challenges as he aged. Maintaining his stamina and physical health in order to perform stunts and fight sequences, as well as to maintain the demanding shooting schedule, was no small feat. There were times when injuries or exhaustion threatened to slow him down, but his dedication to his role and his passion for his work kept him going. His ability to push through physical discomfort and maintain the high standard of his performance was a reflection of his unwavering commitment to his craft.

While there were many obstacles, Mark Harmon experienced several triumphs throughout his career that allowed him to rise above these challenges. One of the greatest triumphs of his career was his role on "NCIS". The success of the show has sealed his place as one of television's most respected actors. The role of Gibbs was transformative, and the show became one of the longest-running and most popular crime dramas in history. His portrayal of the seasoned, no-nonsense NCIS agent resonated with audiences worldwide, earning him widespread acclaim. His natural ability to portray a character with such authority and compassion allowed him to bring depth to the role, making Gibbs not just a law enforcement officer but a figure that viewers could relate to and admire. Harmon's portrayal of Gibbs was one of the key reasons for the show's success, and his leadership both on and off the screen helped foster a tight-knit cast and crew.

The success of "NCIS" was a testament to Harmon's ability to rise to the occasion and meet the demands of a long-running television series. While many shows struggle after several seasons, "NCIS" has remained a top performer for over a decade, largely thanks to the strong performances of its cast, led by Harmon. He is widely regarded as the heart of the show, and the loyalty and commitment he has shown to the series is unmatched. His success with "NCIS" is not only a reflection of his talent but also a testament to his work ethic, professionalism, and the relationships he built with his co-stars. Harmon's ability to stay grounded and continue delivering stellar performances after so many years on the show speaks volumes about his dedication to the craft of acting.

Harmon has enjoyed success in a variety of other projects throughout his career. His roles in "St. Elsewhere" and "Chicago Hope", among others, allowed him to display his versatility as an actor. His ability to transition between different types of roles, demonstrated his wide range of acting skills. These roles allowed him to collaborate with talented directors and actors, further solidifying his reputation as a highly skilled and adaptable actor. Harmon's success across various genres showed that he was capable of taking on diverse roles and excelling in each one, a remarkable achievement that few actors can boast.

His triumphs also extend beyond his professional achievements. He has managed to build a life for himself that is grounded in the values that matter most to him. Throughout his career, he has remained a family man, committed to his wife and children. He has always prioritized his personal life, choosing to keep his family away from the public eye and maintain a sense of normalcy despite the chaos of fame. This decision to keep his private life out of the spotlight is a testament to his integrity and dedication to protecting his loved ones from the pressures of Hollywood. Harmon's ability to keep a strong family foundation while navigating the demands of his career is a triumph in itself, as it is something that many people in the industry struggle to maintain.

Moreover, Harmon's ongoing commitment to philanthropy and community service has been another triumph in his life. Over the years, he has supported various charitable causes and organizations, often using his platform to raise awareness for issues that matter to him. His involvement in charitable work has shown his compassionate nature and his desire to give back to those in need. These contributions, while not always in the public eye, have had a meaningful impact and have further enhanced his legacy as not only a talented actor but also a generous and caring individual.

Mark Harmon's life has been defined by a series of challenges and triumphs that have shaped him both personally and professionally. From overcoming the initial struggles of breaking into Hollywood to handling the pressures of fame and physical demands of acting, Harmon has proven time and again that resilience and determination are key to success.

CHAPTER 11: GLOBAL RECOGNITIONS AND AWARDS

Harmon's career has been marked not only by consistent success but also by significant global recognition and a multitude of prestigious awards. Throughout his journey in the entertainment industry, his exceptional talent, dedication, and contributions to television and film have garnered attention and praise from audiences, critics, and peers alike. These accolades reflect not just his skill as an actor but his broader influence on the television landscape, as well as the respect he has earned from those he has worked with.

The recognition Mark Harmon has received is a testament to his versatility as an actor. He is known for bringing a depth of humanity to his roles, especially in his portrayal of characters who are both tough and vulnerable. This unique balance, coupled with his natural charisma, has made him a standout figure in Hollywood. Over the years, he has been the recipient of numerous awards that honor his achievements and acknowledge the impact of his work on the entertainment industry.

One of the most notable awards in his career came in the form of his recognition for his long-running role as Leroy Jethro Gibbs on "NCIS". The show itself became a cultural phenomenon, with millions of viewers tuning in each week to watch the exploits of the NCIS team. Harmon's portrayal of Gibbs, a seasoned and stoic leader, won him widespread acclaim, and the show's success only helped solidify his place as a household name. Harmon's performance on "NCIS" was celebrated with numerous nominations and wins from prestigious award bodies such as the People's Choice Awards, the Teen Choice Awards, and the TV Guide Awards. These recognitions were reflective of the significant impact "NCIS" had on audiences around the world, and Harmon's portrayal of Gibbs was central to its success.

Harmon also received recognition for his earlier roles, particularly in medical dramas. His performances in "St. Elsewhere" and "Chicago Hope" earned him critical acclaim, and while the recognition was not as widespread during the initial airing of these shows, they contributed to establishing him as a talented and reliable actor in Hollywood. "St. Elsewhere", in particular, is remembered as one of the most iconic and critically acclaimed medical dramas of the 1980s, and Harmon's role as Dr. Robert Caldwell helped earn the series numerous awards. Although he didn't receive an individual award for this performance, the recognition the show garnered served as a testament to the quality of his work.

His career has been punctuated by his ability to consistently deliver high-quality performances, which earned him recognition from various award institutions. The Hollywood community, including his colleagues, took notice of his contributions to the industry, and in recognition of his consistent excellence, Harmon has received accolades that include nominations for Golden Globe Awards, Primetime Emmy Awards, and Screen Actors Guild Awards. These prestigious nominations reflect the high regard in which his work is held, and even though he did not always take home the trophy, the recognition underscored his importance in the entertainment world.

Mark Harmon's recognition is not limited to his acting roles; his behind-the-scenes contributions have also been celebrated. As an executive producer and occasional director, Harmon has played a pivotal role in shaping "NCIS" and ensuring its continued success. His involvement in the development of the show, both in front of and behind the camera, has not gone unnoticed. The success of "NCIS" owes much to his leadership, and his ability to maintain the show's quality and consistency for over a decade was honored by the production industry itself. Harmon's contributions to television have been recognized with nominations and wins at various industry-specific awards ceremonies, which celebrate the technical and creative aspects of television production. International recognition has also played a significant part in Harmon's career. While his fame in the United States has been well-documented, "NCIS" has achieved immense success worldwide, bringing Mark Harmon's talent to audiences in countries across the globe. The show's widespread popularity helped cement Harmon as a globally recognized figure, and his work has been celebrated by international critics and award bodies. Harmon's ability to appeal to a wide range of audiences, regardless of culture or language, speaks to his universal appeal and the depth of his performances. In several countries, "NCIS" became a mainstay of television programming, and Harmon was honored with international awards recognizing his impact on global television.

Perhaps one of the most prestigious recognitions of Mark Harmon's career came in the form of his receipt of the 2008 People's Choice Award for Favorite TV Crime Drama Actor. This particular award was especially meaningful because it was voted on by the public, underscoring the deep connection Harmon had with his audience. Fans of "NCIS" appreciated his portrayal of Gibbs, and this award highlighted his ability to connect with viewers on an emotional level. The People's Choice Award, given by the public, is often seen as a reflection of the actor's true popularity, and this win solidified his status as one of the most beloved figures in television. Over the years, Harmon's reputation as a consistent and dependable actor has earned him numerous accolades within the television community. His achievements have been recognized with nominations for the Primetime Emmy Awards, one of the most coveted honors in the industry. While he did not win an Emmy for his role on "NCIS", his repeated nominations for outstanding performances reflect his standing as one of the top actors in his field. The Emmys are often regarded as the highest form of recognition in the television world, and to be nominated year after year is a true testament to an actor's talent and impact on the medium.

Harmon's philanthropic efforts have also earned him praise and accolades. While he has always been private about his personal life, it is well known that he has been involved in various charitable endeavors. He has supported causes related to military families, children's health, and education, among others. His quiet but impactful contributions to society have earned him respect not only as an actor but as a person who understands the importance of giving back to the community. While these efforts may not be as publicized as his acting career, the recognition Harmon has received for his philanthropic work further solidifies his legacy as a respected figure both in Hollywood and beyond.

Mark Harmon's career has been marked by a series of well-deserved global recognitions and awards that acknowledge his immense talent and contributions to the entertainment world. From his iconic role in "NCIS" to his earlier successes in "St. Elsewhere" and "Chicago Hope", his performances have earned him the respect of both his peers and his audience. His ability to consistently deliver outstanding work, coupled with his behind-the-scenes contributions, has garnered him numerous accolades throughout his career. The recognition he has received, both nationally and internationally, speaks to the enduring impact he has had on television and his ability to connect with audiences across the globe. His journey has been one of hard work, resilience, and excellence, and the awards and honors he has received are a reflection of his status as one of Hollywood's most respected actors.

CHAPTER 12: FAMILY AND FAME

Throughout his career, Mark Harmon has managed to achieve a remarkable balance between his personal life and his professional fame. While his talent and the longevity of his career have garnered him a large and dedicated following, Harmon has always remained deeply rooted in his values, particularly when it comes to his family. For someone who has spent decades in the spotlight, he has been exceptionally private about his personal life, but this doesn't diminish the fact that family has always been at the core of his life, and he has managed to carve out space for both family and the demanding nature of fame.

Mark's approach to fame has always been one of cautious discretion. In an industry that often places a spotlight on personal lives, he has been able to avoid the kind of sensational media coverage that others in his position often face. This privacy, in part, has helped him to maintain a strong connection with his family, keeping them out of the glare of Hollywood's often intrusive eye. His ability to shield his family from public scrutiny has not only allowed him to maintain personal relationships, but it has also ensured that his children and loved ones were not affected by the pressures of fame.

One of the most notable aspects of Mark Harmon's personal life is his long-standing marriage to fellow actress Pam Dawber. The couple, who married in 1987, has managed to keep their relationship largely out of the media spotlight, which has been a rare feat in Hollywood. While they have both enjoyed successful careers in the entertainment industry, they have also valued their privacy and the opportunity to live a more normal life away from the public's eye. Their relationship has been described as one of mutual respect, understanding, and deep affection, which is reflected in their ability to maintain a successful marriage for decades.

Harmon's relationship with Dawber has always been grounded in a sense of partnership, with both individuals focusing on their careers while also prioritizing their family. While Dawber's own career as an actress and producer flourished in the 1980s and 1990s, she stepped away from acting at a certain point to focus on raising their children. This decision was driven by a shared understanding between her and Harmon of the importance of family life. Together, they have raised two sons, Sean and Ty, and despite the demands of their respective careers, they have made sure that their children had a grounded upbringing, far from the pressures of living in the public eye.

Mark and Pam's ability to manage the challenges that come with raising children while simultaneously managing high-profile careers in the entertainment industry speaks to their strong family values. Both have prioritized their children's well-being, ensuring that they were able to grow up with a sense of normalcy, even though their father was a well-known television star. The couple's decision to avoid exploiting their children for publicity is a testament to their desire to keep their family life as private and normal as possible. This choice has helped the Harmon family remain largely insulated from the sometimes overwhelming pressures of fame. Harmon's strong bond with his children has been one of the central elements of his personal life. While his career demanded long hours and extensive travel, he always made an effort to be present for his family. This sense of responsibility and commitment to family has not only shaped his own life but also helped guide his children's paths as they grew up. His children, who have largely stayed out of the public eye, were encouraged to pursue their own passions, but Harmon made sure that they had the necessary support and guidance to navigate the complexities of growing up in a famous family. His commitment to being a father first has made him a respected figure in the eyes of those who know him personally.

Even as his career soared to new heights, Harmon has always managed to keep his fame in perspective. While his roles brought him massive recognition and a dedicated fan base, he never allowed that recognition to overshadow the importance of his family life. He has continuously shown that, for him, personal relationships take precedence over the pressures of fame. In a world where many celebrities have struggled to maintain personal relationships due to the demands of their careers, Mark Harmon has exemplified the ability to balance both worlds successfully.

This balance between family and fame is not only reflected in his actions but also in his public persona. Unlike many of his Hollywood peers, Harmon is not one to seek out the spotlight for personal gain. Instead, he has maintained a level of humility and groundedness, which is rare in an industry that often encourages self-promotion. He has cultivated a reputation for being professional and respectful on set, and this extends to his personal life as well. His ability to remain down-to-earth despite his fame has earned him the admiration of his colleagues and fans alike.

The relationship between Harmon and his wife, Pam Dawber, has also influenced their approach to navigating the pressures of the entertainment industry. Dawber, who is known for her roles in "Mork & Mindy" and "My

Sister Sam", has always been a supportive partner in Harmon's career. While she stepped away from acting to focus on raising their family, Dawber has continued to pursue other creative endeavors behind the scenes. The couple's mutual understanding and support for each other's professional goals have contributed to the longevity of their marriage. Their ability to support one another while managing their individual careers and raising a family is a testament to their strong partnership.

Harmon's commitment to his family is also reflected in the way he handles his work-life balance. While he is known for his dedication to his craft, he has always ensured that his family remains a priority. This approach has allowed him to enjoy the best of both worlds, excelling in his career while maintaining a stable and loving family environment. His ability to manage both has been a source of inspiration to many, proving that it is possible to achieve great success in one's career while also nurturing personal relationships and maintaining a sense of balance in life. Mark Harmon's ability to balance family and fame has been one of the defining aspects of his life and career. His relationship with his wife, Pam Dawber, and his dedication to raising their children in a grounded and private environment, speaks to his values and priorities. Harmon's ability to maintain a successful marriage and family life while navigating the demands of a long and successful career in Hollywood is a rare feat in an industry known for its challenges. His story serves as a reminder that fame does not have to come at the expense of personal relationships, and that with the right balance, one can lead a fulfilling life both professionally and personally.

CONCLUSION

Mark Harmon's journey through life and career offers valuable lessons in perseverance, balance, and dedication. His story is a testament to the power of staying true to one's values while navigating the pressures of fame and success. Over the years, Harmon has consistently demonstrated qualities of humility, professionalism, and unwavering commitment to his family and craft. He has never allowed the allure of Hollywood to overshadow the things that matter most to him, his loved ones, his work, and his sense of integrity. One of the key lessons that emerges from his life is the importance of authenticity. Throughout his career, Harmon has remained true to who he is, both in front of the camera and behind the scenes. In an industry often driven by image and fame, his ability to stay grounded and focused on his core principles has earned him respect and admiration. Rather than seeking attention for the sake of fame, Harmon has chosen to let his work speak for itself. This genuine approach to his career has not only allowed him to achieve lasting success but has also made him a beloved figure among fans and colleagues alike.

Another significant lesson from Harmon's story is the power of balance. While many people in the public eye struggle to juggle their personal and professional lives, Harmon has managed to achieve a rare equilibrium. By maintaining a close-knit family life, staying dedicated to his craft, and focusing on what truly matters, he has set an example of how it is possible to thrive in both personal and professional spheres. His ability to prioritize his family while continuing to build an iconic career is a model of how to live a fulfilling and sustainable life, despite the demands of fame. Mark Harmon's commitment to his family also highlights the importance of support and partnership. His long-lasting marriage to Pam Dawber, along with their shared values, has been a cornerstone of his personal life. This partnership, based on mutual respect, understanding, and shared goals, has been vital to Harmon's ability to stay grounded and focused on what matters most. It is a reminder that the love and support of those closest to us can provide a solid foundation, even amidst the challenges that life presents.

In essence, Mark Harmon's journey is a reminder that true success is not measured solely by career accomplishments or public recognition, but by the integrity and balance one maintains throughout life. His story inspires others to stay true to their values, prioritize what truly matters, and find balance in their own lives. Harmon has shown that a fulfilling career and a strong, supportive family are not mutually exclusive, but rather complementary, creating a life that is not only successful but meaningful.

Made in the USA
Monee, IL
21 November 2024

70824143R00056